First there is a butterfly.
It will soon be a mother.

The mother butterfly lays eggs. She lays the eggs on a plant. The new babies will eat the plant when they are born.

Then, an egg hatches. A
caterpillar comes out.
The caterpillar eats and
grows.

Later, the caterpillar
turns into a pupa.
Inside, it changes.

Next, a butterfly breaks
out of the pupa. It can
fly!

The new butterfly meets
other butterflies. They
fly and eat all day long.
They lay new eggs.

The new eggs will be
new butterflies.

This is the life of a butterfly.